THIS BOOK BELONGS TO:

....

....

JOURNALS BY MOOREA SEAL

the 52 Lists project

52 Lists for Happiness

52 Lists for Togetherness

ALSO BY MOOREA SEAL

Make Yourself at Home

52 Lists
for
Togetherness

JOURNALING INSPIRATION
to DEEPEN CONNECTIONS
with YOUR LOVED ONES

BY MOOREA SEAL

SASQUATCH BOOKS
SEATTLE

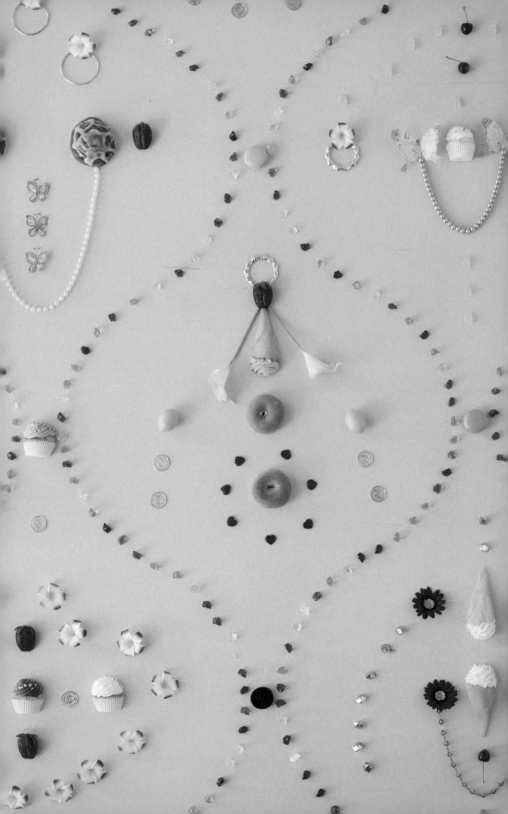

To my treasured friends. Our differences give me courage to celebrate the uniqueness in me and admire the beauty in you. Our similarities fill me with gratefulness, knowing none of us are alone and all are connected. We have constant reason to celebrate and share, simply because we are the individuals that we are. And each day feels sweeter knowing that, for as far into the future as I can see, I get to discover anew who you are as we continually change, adapt, and grow for the better. You are the stars in my night sky.

> "Let there be no purpose in friendship save
> the deepening of the spirit."
> —KAHLIL GIBRAN

If there are two essentials for keeping relationships alive and vibrant, they are curiosity and growth. Just as we as individuals evolve and change over time, so do our relationships. And if we can stay open to discovering new things while respecting and appreciating the consistencies, we are destined to enjoy the bright flickers of new connections, the warm glow of depth and meaning in our relationships, and the sparkle of constant opportunities to love, respect, admire, and appreciate those around us. This book is a little tool of exploration that can meet you right where you are, whether you are looking to develop new friendships, celebrate lifelong friends, explore connections within your family of origin, fall deeper in love with a romantic partner, or engage with your community.

I have been with my husband for more than eight years now. I have known some of my closest friends for over fifteen years, and my connection to my sisters exploded with love and adoration as soon as they were born twenty-three and twenty-eight years ago. The longer you know someone, the more it can feel like you know that person through and through. Familiar with their quirks, routines, passions, and preferences, you may feel like you understand it all. But the truth of the matter is that even as you were growing beside your loved ones and learning about them along the way, they still have ways in which they have been changing and evolving that you have yet to discover! There is always something new to explore within your relationships. Let this collection of lists guide the way to a greater sense of knowing and loving, both within yourself and with your loved ones.

Xo Moorea Seal

Get Together

Now begins the journey to deeper bonds with those cherished people in your life, be they far away or nearby. By picking up this book, opening its pages, and making your first mark, you are joining a greater community of people who are on that same quest toward more meaningful relationships. Whether you are starting this list-making adventure by yourself or filling out your journal alongside one (or more!) of your favorite people, there are so many other people around the world with insight and wisdom to give! Use the hashtag **#52ListsProject** when posting about your lists on social media. What you share may be just the inspiration someone else needs to spark a new connection. And in turn, you may discover that someone else's powerful truth resonates with you as well. Every relationship is one of a kind, and we all have a little magic and insight that can help us grow closer in our one-on-one relationships as well as in our greater communities. Let's create positive change together, one connection at a time.

Learn more about the 52 Lists series at
MooreaSeal.com/pages/52Lists.

Contents

This Is Me

My Community

Togetherness

How To Use This Book

This journal can be filled out in a variety of ways, but the purpose remains the same: each list and Take Action prompt is designed to help you think about your relationships and community and grow closer to those you love. Here are some ideas for ways to use this journal:

- Fill out this book by yourself, one list a week, for the whole year ahead, and reach out to others as the mood strikes you. Some lists and Take Action prompts are made for discussing with others, but what you choose to share is up to you!

- Grab a copy of the book for yourself and another copy for someone you love, and fill out each list side by side! Whether you live near each other or on opposite sides of the world, this book can be a tool for the two of you to check in, learn about each other on a deeper level, and grow closer in your bond one weekly list at a time!

- Gather a group and fill out your lists together, either in person or over social media.

You can fill out each list in order, week by week, if you prefer the structure of starting at the beginning and going through each list consecutively. But if you'd like to mix it up, feel free to jump around, filling out lists in the order they strike your fancy, or try doing one list from each section and continuing that rotation until you've completed the book! It's all up to you to make this journal your own.

This Is Me

TAKE ACTION: Which of these options feel most symbolic of you? Create a crest for yourself, drawing items you circled and objects that best represent who you are.

List 3

LIST EVERYTHING YOU FEEL GRATEFUL FOR
AT THIS PRESENT POINT IN YOUR LIFE.

....

....

....

....

....

....

....

....

TAKE ACTION: Did you include any of your loved ones in this list? This week, focus on your loved ones and your gratefulness for them. Each morning write down one way you are grateful for one person in your life—it doesn't have to be the same person every day. At the end of your week, reflect on how focusing on your appreciation of your loved ones each morning has impacted your days!

List 4

FROM THIS LIST, CIRCLE THE TOP FIVE
WORDS YOU VALUE THE MOST.

PEACE	CONFIDENCE	COMFORT
INDEPENDENCE	GENEROSITY	HAPPINESS
UNITY	BELIEF	FREEDOM
HUMOR	PRIVACY	FAMILY
MONEY	SELF-EXPRESSION	NATURE
LOVE	CONTEMPLATION	HOME
SUCCESS	ADVENTURE	ADAPTABILITY
BEAUTY	CURIOSITY	STRUCTURE
TOUCH	VULNERABILITY	DETERMINATION

1. ....
....
....

2. ....
....
....

3. ....
....
....

4. ....
....
....

5. ....
....
....

List 5

LIST THE WAYS YOUR LIFE IS DIFFERENT
NOW FROM HOW IT WAS ONE YEAR AGO.

....

....

....

....

....

....

....

....

....

TAKE ACTION: Circle the changes that were unplanned or surprises in your life! How have you seen relationships grow because of these changes?

List 6

LIST THE FICTIONAL COUPLES, FRIENDS, AND COMMUNITIES
THAT YOU LOVE FROM BOOKS, MOVIES, AND MEDIA.

....

....

....

....

....

....

....

....

....

TAKE ACTION: Circle the characters who have qualities that you relate to or admire. Do any of the remaining characters remind you of people you know? Write down a few real-life loved ones' names next to the characters that remind you of them!

List 7

LIST THE MANTRAS AND GUIDING
WORDS YOU WANT TO LIVE BY.

....

....

....

....

....

....

....

....

....

....

....

....

....

....

TAKE ACTION: Are any of your loved ones going through a hard time? Choose one of these phrases or mantras that your loved one might need or appreciate, and send them an anonymous letter or postcard with your encouraging words.

List 8

LIST THE ACTIVITIES YOU LIKED TO DO
(BY YOURSELF OR WITH OTHERS) AS A CHILD.

....

....

....

....

....

....

....

....

....

....

TAKE ACTION: Circle which mode of playing was how you liked to play most often as a child.

- Focusing on your own activity by yourself
- Following the lead of a loved one
- Leading or directing an activity
- Working side by side with a friend on your own separate projects
- Building and creating a game or plan in partnership with a friend
- Role-playing characters or performing

Is your answer similar to how you prefer to interact with others now?

List 9

LIST THE ACTIVITIES YOU LOVE DOING ONE-ON-ONE
WITH A LOVED ONE OR IN LARGER GROUPS NOW.

···
···
···
···
···
···
···
···
···

TAKE ACTION: Make a plan this week to do one of your favorite activities with a loved one or a group of friends! Bonus points if you can figure out a way to do an activity that reminds you of your childhood-favorite activities from List 8!

List 10

LIST THE REASONS WHY YOU
SHOULD FEEL PROUD OF YOURSELF.

....

....

....

....

....

....

....

TAKE ACTION: You have reasons to be proud—reasons to love and celebrate you! The best ways to learn to accept love and praise from others is to first accept that love and praise from yourself. This week, review this list every day and say out loud, "I am proud of myself for (fill in the blank)." Practice makes a difference.

List 11

LIST THE NICKNAMES YOU'VE HAD
THROUGHOUT YOUR LIFE.

....

....

....

....

....

....

....

....

....

....

....

....

....

....

....

....

....

....

....

....

....

....

....

....

....

....

....

TAKE ACTION: If you haven't had many nicknames, think of five new ones you'd like to have based on your best and silliest qualities. If you've had lots of nicknames, circle the ones you love and cross out the ones you don't like.

List 12

LIST THE QUALITIES YOU WOULD LIKE TO HAVE IF
YOU WERE A SUPERHERO OR VILLAIN.

List 13

LIST THE THINGS THAT YOU PREFER TO DO ALONE.

....

....

....

....

....

....

....

....

....

....

....

....

....

....

TAKE ACTION: This week, create a little corner of your home that holds a few of the things that are sacred to your "me time." Having space, time, rituals, and practices that are exclusively for you is essential in remembering your individual worth within your relationships.

List 14

LIST ALL OF THE ACTORS WHO WOULD PLAY
CHARACTERS IN THE MOVIE OF YOUR LIFE.

ME: ....

MY ACTOR: ....

MY COMMUNITY: THEIR ACTORS:

....

....

....

....

....

....

....

....

....

....

....

....

MY COMMUNITY:

....

....

....

....

....

....

....

....

....

THEIR ACTORS:

....

....

....

....

....

....

....

....

....

TAKE ACTION: Circle the genre of your life's movie.

Action | Drama | Comedy | Art Film | Mystery
Anime | Musical | Romance | Sci-Fi
Adventure | Coming-of-Age

List 15

LIST YOUR CHILDHOOD FAVORITES AND HAVE
A CLOSE FRIEND DO THE SAME!

Little Me

MEAL: ....

SCHOOL SUBJECT: ....

FEAR: ....

BEST FRIEND: ....

TEACHER: ....

TOY: ....

BOOK: ....

TREAT: ....

GAME: ....

HOLIDAY: ....

SUMMER ACTIVITY: ....

COLOR: ....

MOVIE: ....

SONG: ....

PLACE IN YOUR NEIGHBORHOOD/HOME: ....

Little You

MEAL: ....

SCHOOL SUBJECT: ....

FEAR: ....

BEST FRIEND: ....

TEACHER: ....

TOY: ....

BOOK: ....

TREAT: ....

GAME: ....

HOLIDAY: ....

SUMMER ACTIVITY: ....

COLOR: ....

MOVIE: ....

SONG: ....

PLACE IN YOUR NEIGHBORHOOD/HOME: ....

List 16

LIST THE LESSONS YOU HAVE LEARNED
FROM PEOPLE OLDER THAN YOU.

....

....

....

....

....

....

....

....

....

....

....

....

....

....

....

....

....

....

....

....

....

....

....

....

....

....

TAKE ACTION: If you had to impart one nugget of wisdom to the next generation, what would it be?

....

....

....

....

....

List 17

LIST THE WAYS YOU WOULD DESCRIBE YOURSELF TO
SOMEONE WHO WANTS TO GET TO KNOW YOU AT YOUR CORE.
WHAT UNIQUE QUALITIES MAKE UP YOUR PERSONALITY?

_____

_____

_____

_____

_____

_____

_____

_____

_____

_____

_____

_____

_____

TAKE ACTION: Visit 16Personalities.com and take the quiz to see how your personal preferences inform who you are. If you're interested in seeing how you and your loved ones align or differ, have them take the quiz as well! You might discover some incredible insights.

My Community

"Friendship . . . is born at the moment when one man says to another 'What! You too? I thought that no one but myself . . .'"

—C. S. LEWIS, *THE FOUR LOVES*

———————————

The company we keep so often reflects the people we are. And each of our communities looks different because each one of us is complex in our desires and needs, our experiences of highs and lows in our lives, and how we react to and interact with our diverse set of friends and family. For some, it is easier to gravitate toward one-on-one relationships where delving into deep conversation is the main mode of connection. For others, it feels more natural to find groups of people where activity, lightness, and energy flow with ease. No matter what sort of community involvement feels easiest for you, it's through finding a balance of engaging with others in ways that feel comfortable *as well as* in challenging ourselves to expand in how we interact that we find ourselves feeling truly connected to those around us. It's the unique worlds we create by uniting together with our loved ones that make each relationship feel so special. In this section, you'll be able to reflect on your favorite moments with the ones you love, the things that have brought you together, and the things you value and treasure in your current relationships.

List 18

LIST THE FIRST THINGS THAT COME TO MIND FOR YOURSELF AND FOR SOMEONE YOU LOVE, INSPIRED BY THE PROMPTS BELOW.

Me

COLOR: ....

ANIMAL: ....

SHAPE: ....

SCENT: ....

PLACE: ....

MUSIC GENRE: ....

SKILL: ....

MEAL: ....

MOST LIKELY TO: ....

MAKE OF CAR: ....

AWARD FOR: ....

BOOK: ....

DRINK: ....

MOVIE: ....

You

COLOR: ....

ANIMAL: ....

SHAPE: ....

SCENT: ....

PLACE: ....

MUSIC GENRE: ....

SKILL: ....

MEAL: ....

MOST LIKELY TO: ....

MAKE OF CAR: ....

AWARD FOR: ....

BOOK: ....

DRINK: ....

MOVIE: ....

List 19

LIST THE PLACES WHERE YOUR MOST SIGNIFICANT RELATIONSHIPS GREW.

....

....

....

....

....

....

....

....

....

....

....

....

....

....

....

TAKE ACTION: Write down three locations
where you hope to make new memories!

1. ....

2. ....

3. ....

List 20

LIST THE SPACES AND PEOPLE IN SOCIAL MEDIA
THAT BRING YOU JOY AND INSPIRATION.

....

....

....

....

....

....

....

TAKE ACTION: Community doesn't just happen with the people you know or meet face to face; it's cultivated in any arena where you interact with others often, even just in observation. This week, choose one of the above people in social media or social spaces, and make their page the first place you check in when you engage with social media. An inspiring start in a positive space makes a difference in how you allow online communities to impact you.

List 21

CHOOSE A LOVED ONE AND LIST THEIR
ACCOMPLISHMENTS THAT YOU ARE MOST PROUD OF.

....

....

....

....

....

....

....

....

....

....

....

....

....

TAKE ACTION: Cut up five little pieces of paper. On each of these pieces of paper, write one of the things you are proud of. Hide them, or have someone help you hide them, in various places in your loved one's home so they will discover these notes of affirmation at random.

List 22

CHOOSE SOMEONE CLOSE TO YOU AND LIST THE BOOK, MOVIE, AND TV SHOW CHARACTERS THAT REMIND YOU OF THEM.

TAKE ACTION: Create a drawing of your loved one as if they were the main character in a cartoon based on their life. What would their iconic outfit be? What environment would they be in? Would they have an accessory that they always kept by their side?

List 23

LIST THE THINGS ABOUT YOUR LOVED ONE(S)
THAT YOU WOULD MISS IF YOU DIDN'T SEE
EACH OTHER FOR A LONG TIME.

TAKE ACTION: Write your loved one(s) a letter with all of the reasons why you would miss them if they weren't in your life. Date it, seal the envelope, and give it to them on a day when they are needing a little extra love and comfort.

List 24

CHOOSE SOMEONE CLOSE TO YOU AND LIST
THE DREAMS AND PREDICTIONS YOU HAVE FOR THEM.

....

....

....

....

....

....

....

....

....

....

TAKE ACTION: Ask your loved one how you can best support one of their dreams, and create an action plan to support and inspire them in their goals and aspirations this week!

List 25

LIST ALL OF THE CRUSHES AND ROMANTIC
PARTNERS YOU'VE HAD IN THE PAST.

....
....
....
....
....
....
....
....
....
....
....
....

....

....

....

....

....

....

....

....

....

....

....

....

....

....

....

....

TAKE ACTION: List the top reason(s) why you were drawn to each person next to their name.

List 26

LIST WHAT YOU WOULD BUY FOR YOUR LOVED ONES
IF YOU HAD A MILLION DOLLARS TO SPEND ON THEM.

....

....

....

....

....

....

....

....

....

....

....

....

....

....

....

....

....

....

....

....

....

....

TAKE ACTION: Pick a person to give a gift to this week. Is there a little something you could give that feels like a tiny version of one of your big dream gifts above?

List 27

LIST TEN EASY WAYS THAT YOU CAN CONNECT
WITH YOUR FAVORITE PEOPLE.

....

....

....

....

....

....

....

....

....

....

TAKE ACTION: How many of these things can you fit into one week? Challenge yourself to do one a day or more if you are up for it.

List 28

LIST THE SONGS THAT REMIND
YOU OF A LOVED ONE.

....

....

....

....

....

....

....

....

....

....

....

....

....

TAKE ACTION: What would the playlist title be?
Make a mixtape/playlist or give this list of songs to
your treasured person!

List 29

LIST THE THINGS THAT MAKE YOU FEEL LOVED
AND SUPPORTED BY OTHERS.

LIST THE WAYS YOU LIKE TO LOVE AND SUPPORT OTHERS.

....

....

....

....

....

....

....

....

....

....

....

....

....

....

TAKE ACTION: Take the love languages test at 5LoveLanguages.com/Profile/Singles. Ask one or more of your closest loved ones to take the test and compare your results!

List 30

CHOOSE SOMEONE CLOSE TO YOU AND LIST THE
TIMES YOU HAVE SEEN THEM AT THEIR HAPPIEST.

....

....

....

....

....

....

....

....

....

....

....

TAKE ACTION: Based on your observations, what would be one key ingredient for a happiness boost for your loved one the next time they are feeling blue? Document your observations below.

....

....

....

....

....

List 31

LIST THE WAYS THAT YOU FEEL SIMILAR TO SOMEONE CLOSE TO YOU.

....

....

....

....

....

....

....

....

....

TAKE ACTION: Circle the ways that you immediately felt similar to one another and underline the discoveries that unfolded over the course of your relationship so far.

List 32

LIST THE WAYS THAT YOU FEEL DIFFERENT FROM THE
LOVED ONE YOU WROTE ABOUT IN THE PREVIOUS LIST.

TAKE ACTION: Circle the differences between the two of you that positively benefit and challenge each other. Example: your playfulness helps to give me a break from my seriousness.

List 33

LIST THE TYPES OF MEMORABILIA YOU HAVE HELD ON TO FROM YOUR PAST RELATIONSHIPS, WITH FRIENDS OR FOES, ROMANTIC PARTNERS OR FAMILY.

....

....

....

....

....

....

....

....

....

....

....

....

TAKE ACTION: Take an hour this week to go through the memorabilia that you have held on to—the photos, notes, clothing, emails, whatever it is that acts as a reminder of relationships past. Now is the time to let go of the memories and objects that do not bring you a smile or laugh. Release. Get rid of at least one thing that brings up negative memories and no longer serves you with positive thoughts.

List 34

LIST THE OBJECTS IN YOUR HOME THAT POSITIVELY REMIND YOU
OF YOUR LOVED ONES, INCLUDING THE ONES HERE ON
EARTH AND THE ONES WHO HAVE PASSED ON.

TAKE ACTION: Move one special object or a group of objects into a space in your home where you will see it more often and be reminded of your community. Think of it as a sacred place to honor the special people in your life, the people who are always with you in sentiment and spirit. You're never alone.

togetherness

"Each friend represents a world in us, a world possibly
not born until they arrive, and it is only by
this meeting that a new world is born."

—ANAÏS NIN

_____

From the vast ocean of humanity, you chose the individuals within your community for a reason. Perhaps it was a chance encounter, a blind date, or being born or adopted into the same family that brought you together. In the grand scheme of things, though, it is the decisions you make again and again that not only keep you connected to those in your community but also help you to develop deeper and longer-lasting relationships. Building off the base of self reflection in the first section and contemplation of those in your community in the second section, here you'll find inspiration for ways to reach out to others to spark new opportunities to learn, laugh, go deeper, and feel more connected to those you love. In this section, feel free to choose just one significant person to focus on while writing your lists to strengthen your one-on-one relationship, or explore connections with a few different people in your community, from family to friends to a romantic partner, mixing it up with each list!

List 35

QUIZ ONE OF YOUR LOVED ONES USING THE LIST BELOW.

SWEET or SALTY?

STAY IN or GO OUT?

BEACH, VALLEY, or
MOUNTAINS?

DOGS or CATS?

ORGANIZED or
"INSPIRED MESS"?

OUTGOING or RESERVED?

SPRING, SUMMER, FALL,
or WINTER?

PATIENT or EAGER?

NIGHT OWL or MORNING PERSON?

TRADITIONAL or PROGRESSIVE?

BUILD IT or BUY IT?

PLAYFUL or SERIOUS?

SLOW or FAST?

PAST, PRESENT, or FUTURE?

COMPETITIVE or COOPERATIVE?

TECH or TACTILE?

GROUP or ONE-ON-ONE?

PLAN or JUMP IN?

COFFEE or TEA?

FANTASY or REALITY?

DETAILS or BIG PICTURE?

EARTH, FIRE, WATER, or AIR?

DEBATE or COMPROMISE?

START or FINISH?

LEADER or SIDEKICK?

NOVELTY or CONSISTENCY?

COOK FOOD or ORDER IN?

SUNSHINE, CLOUDS, RAIN,
or SNOW?

TEXT or CALL?

MAXIMAL or MINIMAL?

TAKE ACTION: Compare your loved one's answers to your own list on page 22 (List 2). On the lines below, share the insights you discovered in your similarities and differences! Do any of these similarities and differences impact your lives together?

List 36

LIST WHAT YOUR DREAM VACATION WITH ONE OR
A FEW OF YOUR BEST FRIENDS WOULD LOOK LIKE.

TAKE ACTION: Plan a time to get together with one or a few of your best pals and enjoy one thing from your dream vacation! Even something as simple as an adventure to a new restaurant in your neighborhood can be an experience to savor.

List 37

LIST THE FIRST THINGS YOU BONDED OVER
WITH SIGNIFICANT OTHERS IN YOUR LIFE.

....

....

....

....

....

....

....

....

....

....

....

....

....

....

TAKE ACTION: Circle one of these bonding moments that you haven't experienced lately, and plan a way for you and a loved one to integrate it back into your life via an activity!

List 38

LIST THE INGREDIENTS (ACTIONS, INTENTIONS, ACTIVITIES, AND SENTIMENTS) THAT SUPPORT HAPPY AND HEALTHY RELATIONSHIPS FOR YOU.

TAKE ACTION: In the "pie" above, place the words/phrases that are most important to your relationships in the middle of the circle, and place the least crucial toward the edge.

List 39

IN THE LIST BELOW, FILL IN THE NAME OF THE PERSON
WHO WOULD BE YOUR ADVENTURE BUDDY FOR EACH
ACTIVITY. CIRCLE THE ADVENTURES YOU ACTUALLY WANT
TO MAKE HAPPEN SOMEDAY!

SCUBA DIVE WITH: ....

GO ON A ROAD TRIP WITH: ....

ENTER A PIE-EATING CONTEST WITH: ....

SKI OR SNOWBOARD WITH: ....

GET A TATTOO WITH: ....

BUNGEE JUMP OR SKYDIVE WITH: ....

SWIM WITH DOLPHINS WITH: ....

DYE YOUR HAIR A WILD COLOR WITH: ....

HIKE UP A MOUNTAIN WITH: ....

RIDE AN ELEPHANT WITH: ....

WATCH THE SUNRISE WITH: ....

DANCE IN A PUBLIC PLACE WITH: ....

EXPLORE A FOREIGN COUNTRY WITH: ....

ROCK CLIMB WITH: ....

GO ON A ROLLER COASTER WITH: ....

TAKE ACTION: Imagine you are getting tattoos with your closest friend. Draw the tattoos you would get!

List 40

CHOOSE SOMEONE CLOSE TO YOU, GET TOGETHER,
AND LIST THE SKILL SETS YOU WOULD EACH BRING AS
INDIVIDUALS TO SURVIVING AN APOCALYPSE!

My Skills

Your Skills

....

....

....

....

....

....

....

....

TAKE ACTION: What is one thing you would regret not doing if the world ended tomorrow? Can your loved one help you make this dream come true?

List 41

CHOOSE A LOVED ONE AND LIST THE WAYS THAT
YOUR BACKGROUNDS AND UPBRINGINGS ARE SIMILAR.

....

....

....

....

....

....

....

....

....

....

....

....

....

....

TAKE ACTION: Circle the positive things from both of your pasts that you want to bring with you into your relationship in the future.

List 42

LIST THE WAYS THAT YOUR BACKGROUND AND
UPBRINGING ARE DIFFERENT FROM THE LOVED ONE
YOU WROTE ABOUT IN THE PREVIOUS LIST.

....

....

....

....

....

....

....

....

....

....

....

....

TAKE ACTION: Underline the things in your loved one's background that have influenced you for the better.

List 43

CHOOSE A LOVED ONE, GET TOGETHER, AND
CREATE YOUR SHARED BUCKET LIST.

....

....

....

....

....

....

....

....

TAKE ACTION: Circle one item on your shared bucket list and write out all the steps you will need to take together to make this dream come true. Assign each step based on each of your individual skills and preferences.

List 44

LIST THE WAYS YOU HAVE HELPED YOUR
LOVED ONES THROUGH HARD TIMES.

....

....

....

....

....

....

....

....

....

....

....

....

....

....

....

....

....

....

....

....

....

....

....

....

....

....

....

TAKE ACTION: Take one of your loved ones out to coffee or tea and tell them how much they have helped you in your most challenging seasons of life. Our loved ones sometimes don't know just how much they mean to us until we tell them.

List 45

CHOOSE SOMEONE CLOSE TO YOU AND LIST THE BELIEFS AND
CAUSES THAT YOU BOTH FEEL PASSIONATE ABOUT.

....
....
....
....
....
....
....
....

TAKE ACTION: Research an organization that supports one of your mutual beliefs. Consider donating to this cause with your collaborative time, money, or creativity!

THE CAUSE WE SUPPORT IS: ....

....
....
....
....

List 46

LIST THE MOST MEMORABLE MEALS YOU HAVE HAD WITH A LOVED ONE OR MEMBERS OF YOUR COMMUNITY.

....

....

....

....

....

....

....

....

....

....

....

TAKE ACTION: Did any of these memorable meals have something in common? Was it the ambiance, the setting, the food, an activity, good conversation, or the number of people there that made it feel so special? Take notes from the highlights of each of your favorite meals, and make a plan to host a meal at your home with one of your favorite people or a group of treasured friends/family.

List 47

CHOOSE A LOVED ONE AND LIST THE THINGS THAT
SYMBOLIZE THE VALUE OF WHO THEY ARE TO YOU.

YOU ARE AS STRONG AS: ....

YOU ARE AS VALUABLE AS: ....

YOU ARE AS KIND AS: ....

YOU ARE AS LOVING AS: ....

YOU ARE AS SMART AS: ....

YOU ARE AS FUNNY AS: ....

YOU ARE AS DEEP AS: ....

YOU ARE AS FOCUSED AS: ....

YOU ARE AS JOYFUL AS: ....

YOU ARE AS BEAUTIFUL AS: ....

YOU ARE AS CREATIVE AS: ....

YOU ARE AS POWERFUL AS: ....

YOU ARE AS WISE AS: ....

YOU ARE AS HARDWORKING AS: ....

YOU ARE AS ONE OF A KIND AS: ....

TAKE ACTION: Write a haiku for your loved one, taking inspiration from one or a few of the words you wrote down in the list of symbols. The first line needs to be five syllables; the second, seven syllables; and the third line, five syllables. Then share your affirmations and haiku with them!

List 48

LIST YOUR FAVORITE MOVIES AND TV SHOWS
AND WHO YOU LIKE TO WATCH THEM WITH.

....

....

....

....

....

....

....

....

....

....

....

....

....

TAKE ACTION: If you live near each other, plan a movie night and watch your mutual top favorite together in person! If you live far apart, plan a night to watch your mutual favorite show "together." Start an episode at the same time and text each other to chat along about your favorite moments!

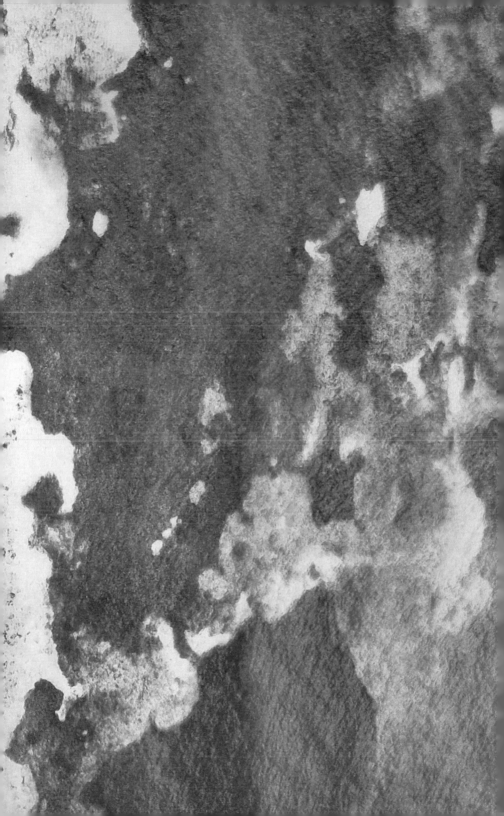

List 49

LIST THE HIGH POINTS AND SUCCESSES YOU
HAVE CELEBRATED WITH YOUR LOVED ONES.

....

....

....

....

....

....

....

....

....

TAKE ACTION: What is one attainable goal that you currently have? Chat with your loved ones about how you can celebrate this goal together once you achieve it, and write your plan here!

MY GOAL: ....

MY NEXT CELEBRATION PLAN: ....

....

....

....

....

....

List 50

CHOOSE A LOVED ONE, GET TOGETHER, AND LIST THE BEST
GIFTS YOU AND YOUR LOVED ONE HAVE EVER RECEIVED.

THE BEST GIFTS I'VE RECEIVED:

....

....

....

....

....

....

....

....

....

....

....

....

THE BEST GIFTS YOU'VE RECEIVED:

....

....

....

....

....

....

....

....

....

....

....

....

TAKE ACTION: Use this list as a reference point the next time you buy or make a gift for your treasured person. Knowing the sorts of sentimental and practical things that make your loved one feel loved makes gift giving more special, and so much easier!

List 51

LIST THE THINGS YOU WOULD PUT IN A TIME CAPSULE
FOR YOUR FAVORITE PERSON TO OPEN IN TWENTY YEARS.

··

··

··

··

··

··

··

··

··

TAKE ACTION: Create your time capsule! Store it in a special box, tape it up so your loved one won't be tempted to open it before it's time, and put a label on the outside with a date and time to open it in the future. Then gift it to your favorite person!

List 52

LIST THE MOST SIGNIFICANT THINGS YOU HAVE
DISCOVERED ABOUT YOURSELF AND YOUR
LOVED ONES THROUGH FILLING OUT THIS JOURNAL!

WHAT I LEARNED ABOUT MYSELF:

**WHAT I LEARNED ABOUT MY
LOVED ONES:**

....

....

....

....

....

....

....

....

....

....

TAKE ACTION: Congratulations on filling up
the pages of your book with stories about the
past and predictions for the future, on explor-
ing who you are and how you and your loved
ones can thrive together, and on following
through with your pursuit of deepening your
relationships. Be sure to revisit these pages as
the years continue, treasuring this time that
you took to deepen your love and respect
for yourself and your community! May your
discoveries stick with you in every new relationship that blossoms in your future.

Further Reading

ON HEALTHY RELATIONSHIPS AND BONDING

Attached: The New Science of Adult Attachment and How It Can Help You Find—and Keep—Love by Amir Levine, MD, and Rachel S. F. Heller, MA

Becoming Attached: First Relationships and How They Shape Our Capacity to Love by Robert Karen, PhD

Dancing with Fire: A Mindful Way to Loving Relationships by John Amodeo, PhD

The Four Loves by C. S. Lewis

Lovingkindness: The Revolutionary Art of Happiness by Sharon Salzberg

MWF Seeking BFF: My Yearlong Search for a New Best Friend by Rachel Bertsche

The Relationship Cure: A 5 Step Guide to Strengthening Your Marriage, Family, and Friendships by John M. Gottman, PhD

Wired for Love: How Understanding Your Partner's Brain and Attachment Style Can Help You Defuse Conflict and Build a Secure Relationship by Stan Tatkin, PsyD, and Harville Hendrix, PhD

ABOUT THE AUTHOR

MOOREA SEAL is a Seattle-based author, retailer, designer, and online curator who is known for her large following on Pinterest and her mental health advocacy. With a desire to empower and uplift people of all ages, she promotes a lifestyle of "Doing Good while Doing Great." Through her fashion and lifestyle brand, also named Moorea Seal, she gives back 7 percent of all proceeds to nonprofits.

Shop her store and learn more at **MooreaSeal.com**.

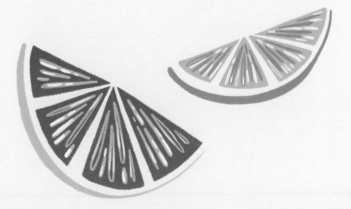

Printed in China

Published by Sasquatch Books

22 21 20 19 18   9 8 7 6 5 4 3 2

Editor: Hannah Elnan
Production editor: Bridget Sweet
Design: Bryce de Flamand
Illustrations: Jordan Kay
Illustrated type: Julia Manchik
Photo styling: Joanna Hawley (cover and pages
42–43, 52–53, 76, 88–89, 108–109, 137)
Photographs: Alisha Johns (pages 4, 63, 79),
Meghan Klein (cover and pages 42–43, 52–53, 76,
88–89, 108–109, 137),
all other photos by Arielle Vey

ISBN: 978-1-63217-219-8

Sasquatch Books
1904 Third Avenue, Suite 710
Seattle, WA 98101
(206) 467-4300
SasquatchBooks.com